THE WONDERFUL WORLD OF WORDS

King Noun and Queen Verb

Dr Lubna Alsagoff
PhD (Stanford)

Marshall Cavendish
Children

King Noun ruled over all the things, people, animals and places in the kingdom — these were the nouns of WOW.

I am King Norman Nautilus Noun. I am the king of WOW.

Queen Verb ruled over all the words that name actions — these were the verbs of WOW.

I am Queen Veronica Vanderbilt Verb. I am the queen of WOW.

The queen wanted to show the king that verbs were just as important to WOW. She waved her hands in the air and spoke loudly.

Verbs of WOW, I order all of you to stop what you are doing!

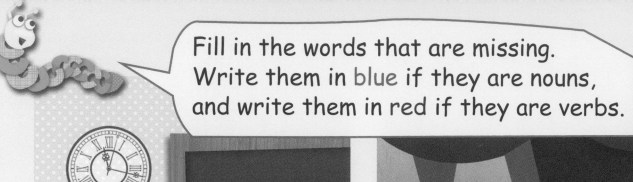

Fill in the words that are missing.
Write them in blue if they are nouns,
and write them in red if they are verbs.

The teacher could not
___ ___ ___ ___ ___ ___.

The dancer could not
___ ___ ___ ___ ___ ___.

Sadly, the ___ ___ ___ ___ could not swim.

The _____ could not play.

The poor little ____ ____ could not run.

Even the ____ ____ could not speak.

The king knew he was wrong.
WOW needed **nouns**.
WOW also needed **verbs**.

When nouns and verbs work together, many wonderful things can happen!

Now the children can _____.

The fox can _____.

The fish can _____.

The _____ can dance.

The _____ can teach!

Can you find other nouns and verbs in the picture that can work together?

Up in the sky, the _____ can _____.

Over the grass, the _____ can _____.

Now that all is well, the _____ can _____.

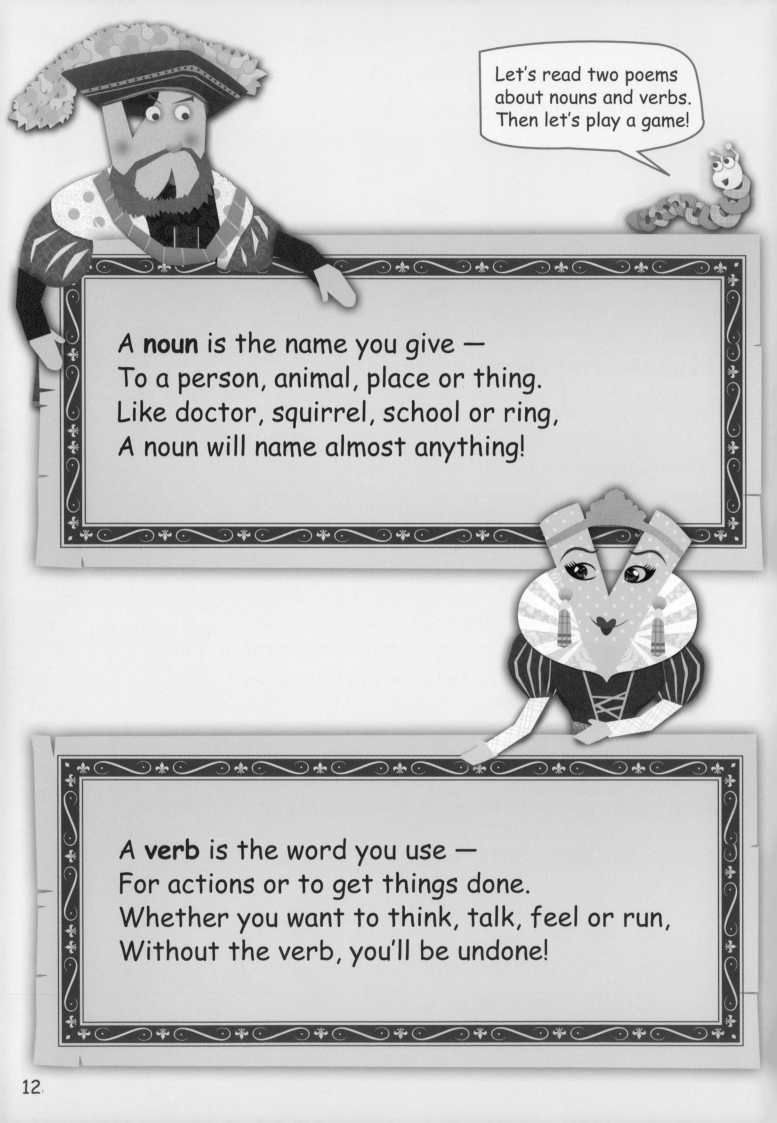

Let's read two poems about nouns and verbs. Then let's play a game!

A **noun** is the name you give —
To a person, animal, place or thing.
Like doctor, squirrel, school or ring,
A noun will name almost anything!

A **verb** is the word you use —
For actions or to get things done.
Whether you want to think, talk, feel or run,
Without the verb, you'll be undone!

 **Noun**

 **Verb**

bird •

• bounce

ball •

• climb

frog •

• fly

squirrel •

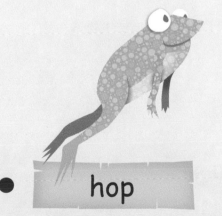

• hop

The Fabulous Forest of WOW

Deep in the forest, far, far from the WOW Castle, Rabbit and Squirrel have finally found Owl!

When Owl, Rabbit and Squirrel get to Donkey's home, they hear very strange sounds.

Donkey just has the hiccups.

Yes, very loud hiccups!

That's true, but wait till you hear what he says after he hiccups!

Donkey is so happy to see Squirrel, Rabbit and Owl.

Oh dear! Every time Donkey hiccups, something happens to his words!

18

Welcome to HICCUP home my .

Oh dear, I only have HICCUP chairs two .

Owl, come and perch at HICCUP table the .

Rabbit, let me take HICCUP hat your .

Would you all like HICCUP tea some ?

Can you help Donkey to say things the right way?

Donkey tells Owl, Rabbit and Squirrel about a strange purple cloud. It made the animals hiccup. The animals then began to say things in a funny way.

tree

ants

garden

table

chairs

clouds

fox

nut

king

donkey

Look for these nouns in the puzzle.

```
G T Y E K N O D X H
W H Q N G X P M R Z
S K N O G A U U O S
C L O U D S R A E Q
L S T N A I T D D C
C H A I R S V K E R
I T R E E F N O U N
G U F Z D T A B L E
D N K I N G Y N S Y
S Y X O F I T T T K
```

Dear Parents,

In this issue, children should notice and learn how nouns and verbs work together to form sentences.

- Help them see the difference between nouns and verbs — nouns name things, while verbs name actions.

- Show them how certain nouns and verbs go together. This is very important when they use grammar to help with their writing. Try getting them to think of more verbs that go with a particular noun. For example, can they think of what else a frog can do? Frogs can swim, they can croak, some can even climb trees!

Page	Possible Answers
8–9	teach/think
	dance/twirl
	fish
	children
	fox
	king
11	play/laugh
	run/prance
	swim/jump
	dancer/girl
	teacher/man
	sun/shine | bird/fly
	fox/run | frog/hop
	children/play
13	bird = fly | ball = bounce | frog = hop | squirrel = climb
19	my home | two chairs | the table | your hat | some tea